Railways & Recollections 1976

Contents

Introduction	3
InterCity 125 takes to the tracks	4
The Lyme Regis branch revisited	8
Destination Derby	10
A walk around Waterloo	14
A summer's day in Somerset	17
Catch it while you can: the 'Westerns South Western'	20
The busy scene at Clapham Junction	21
The great way west	24
Underground interlude	34
Nostalgia at the Bluebell Railway	37
As it was in the beginning…	40
A saunter round the Southern	41
1976 Happenings (1)	7
1976 Happenings (2)	25
1976 Arrivals & Departures	16
No 1 Records	31
TV favourites	46

Silver Link Publishing Ltd
The Trundle
Ringstead Road
Great Addington
Kettering
Northants NN14 4BW

Tel/Fax: 01536 330588
email: sales@nostalgiacollection.com
Website: www.nostalgiacollection.com

© Chris Harris 2014
Photographs by Ray Ruffell © *The NOSTALGIA Collection* archive, unless otherwise credited

All rights reserved. No part of this publication may be reproduced, stored in a retrieval system or transmitted, in any form or by any means, electronic, mechanical, photocopying, recording or otherwise, without prior permission in writing from Silver Link Publishing Ltd.

First published in 2014
British Library Cataloguing in Publication Data

A catalogue record for this book is available from the British Library.

Introduction
The year of the heatwave

The year 1976 will long be remembered for the remarkable hot and dry summer that we enjoyed. The summer of 1975 had also been warm and dry; this was followed by a dry winter, and although 1976 started with severe gales in early January, the spring of that year was generally mild and dry too. May was pleasant, but it was during June that the hot weather really started. Between 23 June and 7 July inclusive the temperature reached 90 degrees Fahrenheit every day in England, peaking on Saturday 3 July with a high of 97 degrees Fahrenheit in Cheltenham. The high temperatures continued throughout July and for almost all of August, by which time the drought conditions were becoming a problem, parts of the country having had no rain for 45 days. Rivers and reservoirs were drying up, and in some areas water shortages were so severe that household supplies had to be collected from standpipes. Serious damage was done by heath and forest fires, especially in southern England. The Government appointed Dennis Howell as 'Minister for Drought' to oversee what was becoming a serious crisis – then a series of thunderstorms (just in time for the August bank holiday weekend) brought the

ISBN 978 1 85794 431 0

Printed and bound in the Czech Republic

Title page: **CHESTER** The time is 1110 on Thursday 29 July 1976, and a traveller beginning a journey waves farewell to friends as the train pulls out of Chester station. Known as Chester General until 1969, the station dates from 1848 and was built by Thomas Brassey to a design by Francis Thompson. Like the departing traveller, let us also take a journey around the British Rail network in 1976…

Introduction

heatwave and the drought to a close; rainfall during the autumn of 1976 was much higher than average, and water reserves were soon replenished.

The glorious summer weather helped take our minds off the political and economic situation, which was not good with inflation averaging more than 16%. In March Prime Minister Harold Wilson announced his resignation with effect from 5 April; his place was taken by James Callaghan, who had defeated Roy Jenkins and Michael Foot in the resulting Labour leadership contest. By this time the position of the pound on the currency markets had slipped to a value of $1.90 – the first time it had fallen below $2 – and the slide continued, by early June dropping almost to $1.70. Although it rallied to around $1.80 for the rest of the summer, a further decline followed, with the pound slipping to $1.68 on 27 September. Two days later it was announced that Britain was applying for a loan from the International Monetary Fund. After negotiations between the Government and the IMF the loan was agreed in mid-December; one consequence was the requirement for unpopular cuts in public expenditure, although by the end of the year the pound had recovered to an exchange rate above $1.70.

Meanwhile the Liberal leader, Jeremy Thorpe, had resigned on 10 May following allegations about his private life, and David Steel became leader of the Liberal Party on 7 July. In the Royal Family it was announced that Princess Margaret and Lord Snowdon were to separate after 16 years of marriage.

The FA Cup Final on 1 May produced a surprise result when Second Division Southampton beat Manchester United 1-0, the single goal being scored by Bobby Stokes in the 83rd minute.

The pop music scene was shaken by the arrival of punk rock, while a couple of the more outré exhibitions at the Institute of Contemporary Arts in London were denounced by the tabloid press.

On the railways, although a Government transport policy consultation paper issued in April raised fears of possible further cuts, a more encouraging development was the introduction of the InterCity 125 High Speed Train on the route from London to Bristol and South Wales from Monday 4 October. The new trains and faster schedules were warmly welcomed by the travelling public, and ridership on this route increased significantly.

Please now join me as we take a nostalgic tour of the railway network during the year of the hot summer, when the average house price in the UK was £12,700 and a gallon of petrol cost 76p…

Chris Harris, Poole, Dorset.

WINDSOR Happy in his work and clutching what is almost certainly a railway magazine in his left hand, Ray Ruffell leans from the guard's van of a BR standard-design EPB suburban unit at Windsor & Eton Riverside station in April 1976.

InterCity 125 takes to the tracks

London to Bristol and South Wales was being upgraded to allow 125mph running wherever possible. Deliveries of the new units commenced in the spring of 1976, and numerically the first of the production batch, unit No 253 001, is seen while on test at Reading on Friday 7 May.

Below: **READING** A close-up of the power car at the other end of unit No 253 001 on the same day illustrates the prominent branding applied to these trains when new. The production InterCity 125 units were attractively shaped, with a distinctive 'nose cone'. Many are still in service at the time of writing – 37 years after introduction and now wearing very different liveries – but their design has not aged and they still cut a dash as they speed through the countryside. The shape of what in 1976 were things to come can be compared with diesel-hydraulic locomotive No 1010 *Western Campaigner*, which is entering Reading station with the 1025 service from Birmingham. Built at BR Swindon Works and entering traffic in October 1962, *Western Campaigner* was preserved after withdrawal in February 1977 and in 2013 can be seen on the West Somerset Railway.

Above: **READING** Without question, the most significant railway event of 1976 was the introduction of InterCity 125 High Speed Trains into regular service. A prototype high-speed diesel train had been built at BR Derby Works in 1972; test running on the East Coast Main Line had commenced the following year, and in May 1975 the prototype entered revenue service running between London Paddington and Bristol. By 1975 27 production InterCity 125 units were in build, while the route from

Inter City 125 takes to the tracks

Right: **CHIPPENHAM** From Monday 9 August 1976 some of the new InterCity 125 units started to be used in passenger service on the Western Region, albeit running on existing schedules. Unit No 253 001 is seen again, this time forming a down service at Chippenham two days later on Wednesday 11 August. Note the platform staff loading parcels into the train's van area from a platform trolley; in 1976 the railways still operated a significant parcels service. *Brian Jackson*

Below: **READING** With the introduction of the winter timetable from Monday 4 October 1976 the InterCity 125 units started running to high-speed schedules on the London-Bristol-Swansea route, with a saving of 23 minutes over the previous best London to Cardiff time. Unit No 253 004 is coming into Platform 4 at Reading on the first day of the new timetable. The severe straight sides and box-like front end of 'Tadpole' unit 1201, waiting to depart for Redhill and Tonbridge in the bay platform on the left, look rather dated by comparison – nonetheless these rugged and reliable units provided an excellent service on this route for a number of years, intensive diagramming meaning that they averaged around 11,000 miles every four weeks, with five out of the six units required each day to maintain the timetable.

PADDINGTON InterCity 125 unit No 253 003 enters London Paddington station on Saturday 16 October ready to form the 1100 service to Swansea. It will be noted that there are two catering vehicles included in the formation – as delivered, the units had both a buffet car and a kitchen car, a provision that was later regarded as extravagant for the relatively short journey times between London and Bristol/South Wales. Nonetheless the reduction in on-board catering, and in particular the withdrawal of the full meal service that was once such an enjoyable feature of long-distance rail travel, is a development that has not met with the approval of all passengers; however, it is encouraging to note that in 2013 First Great Western has reintroduced restaurant cars, featuring delicious menus devised by Mitch Tonks, on a couple of Paddington-Plymouth and Plymouth-Paddington journeys on Mondays to Fridays.

NEWPORT Unit No 253 003 is seen again on the same day after arrival at Newport as the 1100 service from Paddington. The introduction of these stylish new trains to this route in 1976 was timely; for some years the parallel M4 motorway had been abstracting passenger traffic on the London-Bristol/South Wales corridor, but the new rail service with improved comfort and shorter journey times quickly reversed this trend, with ridership increasing by 15% in the first six months from the introduction of the new trains. Within two years passenger numbers on this route were up by 33%, amply justifying the marketing strapline that had been applied to the revised service: 'It's the changing shape of rail'.

Inter City 125 takes to the tracks

1976 Happenings (1)

January
- Hurricane-force winds cause millions of pounds worth of damage across UK; at Worcester pinnacle from main tower crashes through roof of cathedral.
- British and Icelandic ships clash at sea in 'Cod War'.
- First commercial flight by Concorde.

February
- National Exhibition Centre, near Birmingham Airport, is opened by Her Majesty the Queen.
- At Winter Olympics at Innsbruck, Austria, skater John Curry wins gold medal for Great Britain.
- 'Cod War' causes Iceland to break off diplomatic relations with Great Britain.

EASTBOUND FROM NEWPORT
Passenger carriages in the InterCity 125 units were built to the British Railways Standard Mark 3 design, which had first appeared in locomotive-hauled sets on the electrified routes from London Euston in 1975. With their bright and cheerful interiors incorporating a mixture of facing and 'airline'-style seating, together with air-conditioning, these commodious carriages played a major role in the success of the new service – and the new image for British Rail. Illustrating the spacious comfort of an 'airline'-style seat in what was then still called 2nd Class, seven-year-old Margaret Ruffell enjoys a snack collected from the buffet car while returning from Newport to London Paddington on Saturday 16 October.

March
- Production of Hillman Imp cars ends (after 13 years).
- Harold Wilson announces resignation as Prime Minister, effective from 5 April.
- Princess Margaret and Lord Snowdon announce that they will separate (they have been married for 16 years).

April
- James Callaghan becomes Prime Minister, having defeated Roy Jenkins and Michael Foot in Labour Party leadership contest.
- Resignation of Cabinet Minister John Stonehouse leaves Government without majority in House of Commons.

May
- Southampton beat Manchester United 1-0 at Wembley to win FA Cup.
- Jeremy Thorpe resigns as leader of Liberal Party.

June
- 'Cod War' between Great Britain and Iceland ends.
- Steadily increasing temperatures herald heatwave and drought – by 25 June temperatures are exceeding 95°F, and remarkable summer weather continues until almost end of August.
- Seychelles become independent of the UK.

The Lyme Regis branch revisited

Above: **LYME REGIS** The branch from Axminster to Lyme Regis had a life of just over 62 years, being opened in August 1903 and closed in November 1965. The terminus at Lyme Regis was situated around three-quarters of a mile from the town centre and at the top of a steep hill from the town. When Brian Jackson visited in July 1976, the wooden station buildings had survived well despite more than ten years of disuse, although the prolific buddleia had made considerable encroachment. Fortunately this building has been saved; it was dismantled in 1979 and reused to provide the 'West Country Buffet' at Alresford on the 'Watercress Line' heritage railway. The former station site at Lyme Regis is now in light industrial use, and all evidence of the buildings and platform has been removed. *Brian Jackson*

Below: **CANNINGTON VIADUCT** This ten-arch viaduct, 600 feet long and with a maximum height of 92 feet, still survives and is now a listed structure, being one of the earliest viaducts to have been built in concrete. This photograph, also taken in July 1976, clearly shows the jack arch added owing to the greensand and unstable nature of the ground in the area. In 2013 the viaduct is one of the few tangible remains of the branch; another is one of the three celebrated 4-4-2 Radial tanks that worked this line for many years – No 30583 (488) is preserved on the Bluebell Railway in Sussex. *Brian Jackson*

COMBPYNE The Axminster-Lyme Regis branch had been single-track throughout, except for a passing loop at the remote Combpyne station. Operation of the branch had passed from the Southern Region to the Western Region of British Railways in January 1963, and in November of that year diesel multiple units (normally a single car during the winter months) took over from steam traction, but notwithstanding this modernisation and economy the branch was closed in November 1965. This was unsurprising as, except during the peak holiday season, loadings were very light – and during the winter sometimes averaged as few as between three and seven passengers per train. Nonetheless, during 1974 an ambitious scheme was launched by preservationists to reopen the branch using a 1ft 3in-gauge light railway, and work began at the former Combpyne station. Around half a mile of track was laid and rolling stock was acquired second-hand from the Longleat Railway in Wiltshire, but construction work was never completed and when these photographs were taken on Thursday 8 July 1976 work on the grand-sounding 'Axe and Lyme Valleys Light Railway' had ceased. The stock was later dispersed to other attractions. *Brian Jackson*

Destination Derby

DERBY The 08 Class diesel shunter was the very successful principal replacement for the many tank locomotives that had been used on shunting duties throughout British Railways. A total of 966 of these diesel shunters were built by the British Railways works at Crewe, Darlington, Derby and Doncaster between 1952 and 1962, making it the most numerous locomotive class on the system. This example, No 08333, was built at Derby Works and entered traffic in November 1957. At work close to where it was built, it was photographed on Friday 16 July 1976 from the platform at Derby station moving a short rake of empty stock consisting of a BG, a Travelling Post Office and two British Railways Standard Mark 1 carriages. This locomotive was in service for just over 25 years, being withdrawn in December 1982. *Brian Jackson*

DERBY A three-car Class 104 diesel multiple unit stands in Derby station on the same day. Built by the Birmingham Railway Carriage & Wagon Company, the Class 104 units entered traffic from April 1957 and a number remained in service into the 1990s; several survive in preservation. Further along the platform we see a three-car Class 120 unit built by British Railways Swindon Works in 1958 for what were described as cross-country services; as built, the centre trailer had contained a small buffet area. Withdrawal of the Class 120 units was completed by the autumn of 1989, and unfortunately only one trailer carriage has entered preservation.

In January 1941 Derby station had been one of the few locations in the city to be severely damaged by bombing during the Second World War; the platform buildings, canopies and footbridge were rebuilt in 1952 using pre-stressed concrete, giving the station a functional yet distinctive aspect, as seen from this photograph. The canopies have since been replaced, considerably changing the appearance of the station. *Brian Jackson*

DERBY Signal boxes sometimes carried interesting names – some quite grand-sounding – and on the Great Western the title almost always ended with the words 'Signal Box'. However, in some places quite succinct titles were used, as epitomised by the old Midland Railway 'Engine Sidings No 2' box photographed at Derby on Friday 16 July; a perfect example of a standard Midland Railway box and the railway modeller's Airfix kit. Derby power signal box had opened in 1969, resulting in the closure of around 40 signal boxes in the area, although Engine Sidings No 2 remained open to maintain access between the station and the diesel depot. With the increase of fixed-formation high-speed trains on passenger services, the need for locomotive changes at Derby declined; Engine Sidings No 2 box closed in 1987 and subsequently demolished. *Brian Jackson*

DERBY Situated within the railway works complex at Derby was the old Midland Railway roundhouse, and when this photograph was taken in February 1976 it was in use to repair breakdown cranes. Derby Works was scaled down from the early 1980s, many of the buildings being demolished and the land used for Derby's Pride Park business area. However, some of the original 1839 Midland Railway buildings, including the roundhouse, were given Grade 2 listed status, and today form the Roundhouse Campus of Derby College. The Campus was officially opened by HRH The Princess Royal in October 2010, and the roundhouse building itself is used as a social area and cafeteria. *Brian Jackson*

Below: **DERBY** This former Midland Railway Johnson 0-6-0 1F tank locomotive, No 1708 (BR No 41708), was built at Derby in 1880, and had the distinction of becoming the oldest operational locomotive in service on British Railways; allocated to Barrow Hill, Chesterfield, it was withdrawn in December 1966. Preserved after withdrawal and now the sole survivor of a class of 262 locomotives, this fine veteran had received attention at Derby Works in February 1976. At the time of writing it resides on home ground as part of the Barrow Hill Roundhouse collection. *Brian Jackson*

Above: **DERBY** A selection of diesel-electric locomotives photographed standing outside Derby Works in February 1976 reminds us of the motive power that was in general use during that era. At the front is Class 45 No 45123, built at British Railways Crewe Works, which entered service in June 1962 as D52 and was withdrawn in July 1987. The Class 25 locomotive behind it, No 25111, was built at Derby Works in April 1964 as D5261, and remained in service until March 1980. Beyond that is one of the 36 Class 25 locomotives that were built by Beyer Peacock; No 25298 dates from April 1966 and was withdrawn in March 1985. Next in line, No 25015, had been condemned in December 1975 and was therefore officially withdrawn when this photograph was taken, although it was not scrapped until January 1977; it had been built at British Railways Darlington Works and entered traffic in October 1961 as D5165. Bringing up the rear is Class 45 No 45033, which had been built at Derby and entered traffic in July 1961 as D39; it was withdrawn in February 1988. *Brian Jackson*

Above: **DERBY** Photographed from the yard of the Trent Motor Traction bus garage backing onto the railway on Friday 27 February, Class 45 diesel-electric locomotive No 45057 departs northwards with a train consisting mainly of British Railways Standard Mark 2 stock. This locomotive was built at British Railways Crewe Works and entered traffic in March 1961 as D93; it was withdrawn from service in January 1985. *Brian Jackson*

Right: **DERBY** During the early hours of Wednesday 14 July 1976 Trent suffered a major fire at its Derby garage that resulted in the loss of 39 vehicles, with severe damage to seven others. Among those destroyed were seven brand-new buses – two Leyland National single-deckers, two Bristol VRT double-deckers and three Leyland AN 68 double-deckers. In this photograph, taken two days later, the remains of fleet number 464 (64 ACH), a Leyland Atlantean with a 74-seat Weymann body, can be seen on the left. Next to it what had been a new Bristol VRT double-decker has been totally destroyed, while several ruined Leyland National single-deckers can also be seen. Fitters are examining the wreckage to see if anything can be recovered from this scene of destruction. *Brian Jackson*

A walk around Waterloo

Below: **WATERLOO** Built in 1971-72, the experimental PEP units were used in passenger service from 1973. They brought the benefits of sliding-door stock to Southern Region commuters for the first time, but the reduction in the number of seats compared with the traditional compartment stock then widely used on the Southern suburban routes meant that passengers reacted with mixed feelings. While the General Manager decoded PEP as 'People's Extremely Popular', many regular users felt that 'Pack 'Em Perpendicular' was more accurate. In service these experimental units were used mainly on the routes from London Waterloo to Hampton Court, Shepperton or Chessington South. 4PEP unit No 4001 is seen here leading a PEP formation departing from Waterloo for Hampton Court on Wednesday 25 February 1976. The PEP units were withdrawn from service later in 1976, having played an important role in evaluating designs for the next generation of suburban stock.

Above: **WATERLOO** By 1976 most services on the Waterloo to Portsmouth line were in the hands of the 4CIG and 4BIG units built at British Railways York Works in 1970-72. They were very similar to the CIG/BIG units that had been built for the London Victoria-Brighton/Eastbourne lines in 1964-66, with the exception that the passenger seating was less comfortable on these later units, with thinner cushions and a lack of wing pieces in the open 2nd Class saloons. Compared with the 1937 COR/BUF stock that these units had replaced on the Waterloo-Portsmouth fast trains, the carriage interiors looked bright and modern, but many users felt that the old stock had provided more comfortable seating. Seen at Waterloo on Wednesday 25 February, 4CIG units 7387 (left) and 7345 (right) epitomise Portsmouth line trains in 1976.

Above: **WATERLOO** The scene illustrated in this photograph was completely swept away in the early 1990s when the Waterloo Eurostar terminus was built on this site. Electro-diesel locomotive No 74001 has a train consisting of just one empty milk tank at Waterloo north sidings on Saturday 13 March 1976. The electrification of the line from Waterloo to Bournemouth in 1967 had produced a requirement for a few more powerful electro-diesel locomotives for such workings as ocean liner services to Southampton Docks. Ten electric locomotives from the batch of 24 originally built for the Kent Coast electrification were therefore modified to become electro-diesels. This locomotive was originally built at British Railways Doncaster Works as E5015 and entered traffic in February 1960; after temporary withdrawal for conversion, it re-entered service as an electro-diesel in February 1968. It was withdrawn in December 1977.

Above right: **WATERLOO** The Southern Railway announced in January 1935 that it planned to spend £500,000 on resignalling and improving the lines running into London Waterloo. An important feature would be the installation of colour light signalling, with a new signal box at the terminus. Constructed from concrete, the new signal box contained a total of 309 levers, in three frames to control the main local, main through and Windsor lines. The change to the new signalling was made in the early hours of Sunday 18 October 1936, when the 0035 to Hampton Court was the final train to be signalled away from the terminus by semaphore signals; the 0130 to Salisbury departed under the control of colour lights. Still looking smart and modern after nearly 40 years of use, the 1936 signal box was photographed on Wednesday 25 February 1976.

1976 Arrivals & Departures

Births

Marsha Thomason	Actress	19 January
Emma Bunton	Musician	21 January
Keeley Hawes	Actress	10 February
Chris Hoy	Champion cyclist	23 March
Clare Buckfield	Actress	10 April
Martine McCutcheon	Actress and musician	14 May
Ross Noble	Comedian	6 June
Ellen MacArthur	Yachtswoman	8 July
Anna Friel	Actress	12 July
Lisa Riley	Actress	13 July
Geraint Jones	Cricketer	14 July
Naomie Harris	Actress	6 September
Tina Barrett	Musician	16 September
Cat Deeley	Television presenter	23 October
Stephen Craigen	Footballer	29 October
Dominic Monaghan	Actor	8 December

Deaths

Agatha Christie	Writer	(b1890)	12 January
Margaret Leighton	Actress	(b1922)	13 January
L. S. Lowry	Artist	(b1887)	23 February
Bernard Montgomery	Field Marshal	(b1897)	24 March
Colin MacInnes	Writer	(b1914)	22 April
Keith Relf	Musician	(b1943)	14 May
Sybil Thorndike	Actress	(b1882)	9 June
Sir Stanley Baker	Actor	(b1928)	28 June
Alastair Sim	Actor	(b1900)	19 August
Edith Evans	Actress	(b1888)	14 October
Benjamin Britten	Composer	(b1913)	4 December

WATERLOO The 1936 signal box can be seen in the background of this photograph taken by Ray Ruffell from a train arriving at the terminus on a sunny day in August 1976. On the left a 4EPB unit dating from 1953 and built to an SR Bulleid design is setting out from Waterloo; this unit has retained suburban blue livery. The 1968-built 4VEP unit leading the train alongside the EPB is in blue and grey livery despite the 2nd Class accommodation being little different from suburban stock, although the VEPs were gangwayed throughout and did include some 1st Class compartments.

A summer's day in Somerset

Right: **CHARD JUNCTION** station was opened to traffic as Chard Road in 1860; it was located just over 3 miles south of Chard, and a rail link to the town itself was opened three years later. At what consequently became known as Chard Junction, the platform for the branch was in the station yard rather than the more usual arrangement of a bay beside one of the through platforms. Chard Junction station was closed to passengers in March 1966, and sections of what had been the LSWR and Southern main line from Waterloo to Exeter were singled two years later; a passing loop was retained at Chard Junction although trains no longer called at the station. On Thursday 12 August 1976 a service from Exeter to Waterloo passes through the closed station headed by 'Crompton' Class 33 diesel-electric locomotive No 33007; built by the Birmingham Railway Carriage & Wagon Company and entering traffic in May 1960 as D6507, this locomotive remained in service with British Rail until December 1986. *Brian Jackson*

Left: **CHARD JUNCTION** As a diesel multiple unit approaches and runs into the loop at Chard Junction with a down train, we see a scene of interesting comparisons: the former LSWR line to the West of England reduced to a single track with passing loops, a crossing controlled by barriers and gantry-mounted electric signals, and the signals controlled from a signal box dating from 1875. The train is formed of a Class 119 unit built by the Gloucester Railway Carriage & Wagon Company in 1959. These 28 three-car 'Cross Country' units were designed to provide comfortable passenger accommodation for medium to long-distance journeys, and most of the batch were in service until the late 1980s, the final examples remaining until 1995. *Brian Jackson*

CHARD JUNCTION The 1875-vintage LSWR signal box at Chard Junction is seen in close-up on Thursday 12 August 1976. Housing a 15-lever Stevens frame and gate wheel, this venerable building remained in use until 11 September 1982, when the structure was found to be unstable. A temporary panel was used until a permanent replacement building was provided in December 1982. With the opening of a 3-mile loop at Axminster from 11 December 2009, a new NX panel was installed in the 1982 building; this was in use until the area was brought under the control of Basingstoke panel from 11 March 2012, and the 2009 NX panel can now be seen at Yeovil Railway Centre. Class 159 diesel multiple units provide a good service between London and Exeter along this line in the 21st century, but do not call at Chard Junction, which remains closed. *Brian Jackson*

CHARD JUNCTION Sidings for a creamery were installed on the south side of the line at Chard Junction in 1937. Shunting milk tanks in what was then the United Dairies siding on the same day as the previous photograph is 0-4-0 diesel-mechanical shunter No 12. Built by Ruston & Hornsby in 1951, No 12 had previously been at the Windsor Street gas works in Birmingham before moving to Chard Junction in 1974; it has since been preserved on the Cholsey & Wallingford Railway. Note the Bedford TK lorries in the background, which were a popular choice by many hauliers in the 1970s; in the 21st century the Bedford marque, once widely seen on lorries and coaches throughout Britain, no longer exists. The creamery sidings at Chard Junction were closed in 1980. *Brian Jackson*

CHARD JUNCTION The line from Chard Junction to Chard Central (and onwards to Taunton) was closed in September 1962. Taken from the trackbed of this former branch line, this photograph shows that the name board on the old branch platform still survived almost 14 years after closure. The cast concrete board was a typical product of the Exmouth Junction concrete works, whose range of output knew few bounds. The creamery can be seen in the background, on the other side of the Waterloo-Exeter line. *Brian Jackson*

CHARD CENTRAL station opened in September 1866 as the terminus of a broad-gauge branch from the Bristol & Exeter Railway at Taunton. The station was run by the Great Western Railway from 1876, and served by LSWR trains from Chard Junction shortly afterwards (the LSWR Chard Town station was closed to passengers in 1917), although through running between Chard Junction and Taunton was not possible until the GWR line onwards from Chard Central was converted to standard gauge in 1891. Although the line from Chard Junction to Taunton was closed to passengers in September 1962 and to goods traffic in July 1964, Chard Central station was fortunately not demolished and when photographed in August 1976 this classic example of a Victorian country station was in use as a bitumen distribution depot. Like the station, the Reliant Regal van seen in the right foreground would also now be a classic, as few remain on the roads today. *Brian Jackson*

Catch it while you can: the 'Westerns South Western'

MELDON QUARRY After the glorious summer, Saturday 30 October 1976 was a day of dull weather, but this did not dampen the enthusiasm of those travelling on the 'Westerns South Western' railtour. The special, formed of 12 British Railways Standard Mark 1 carriages, left London Paddington at 0825 and travelled via the former Great Western West of England main line to Exeter, then continued via the old LSWR Exeter-Plymouth line to Meldon Quarry, where arrival was just after midday. The two Class 52 diesel-hydraulic locomotives, both built at BR Swindon Works, are seen running round their train after arrival. No 1009 *Western Invader* entered service in September 1962 and was scrapped following withdrawal in November 1976, while No 1023 *Western Fusilier*, which entered service in September 1963, was withdrawn in February 1977 and subsequently preserved; in 2013 it is on display at the National Railway Museum at York. The line between Meldon and Bere Alston had been closed in May 1968, thus severing the former LSWR and Southern Railway main line to Plymouth. *Brian Jackson*

CREDITON The returning 'Westerns South Western' railtour is seen approaching Crediton. Already the level crossing gates here have been replaced by lifting barriers, although the LSWR Type 1 signal box dating back to the late 1870s remains; another sign of the times is the car scrapyard beside the line. The return working of the railtour was via the old LSWR and Southern Railway route from Exeter via Salisbury to Basingstoke, then continuing via Mortimer and Southcote Junction to Reading and thence via the former Great Western main line to Paddington. *Brian Jackson*

The busy scene at Clapham Junction

CLAPHAM JUNCTION Dating from 1907, Clapham Junction A signal box was situated on a girder bridge just beyond the London end of the station. During the Second World War an additional roof of steel sheeting was erected over the box as an air raid precaution. This protective sheeting remained until the bridge carrying the box partially failed during the morning peak period on Monday 10 May 1965, resulting in the closure of Waterloo for the rest of that day while repairs were carried out. The steel sheeting was subsequently removed, although the girder framework was left, and can be clearly seen in these photographs. Carrying headcode 58 and leading a Waterloo to Windsor service, 2EPB unit No 5791 approaches Clapham Junction station on Wednesday 28 April 1976. This was one of a batch of 15 such units built at Eastleigh in 1954-55 for use between Newcastle and South Shields; they passed to the Southern Region when the South Tyneside system was de-electrified in 1963, and were easily recognised by the larger brake vans when compared with the EPB units originally intended for the Southern.

The second photograph taken at the same spot on the same day shows Class 33/1 diesel-electric locomotive No 33111 and a 4TC unit approaching Clapham Junction station with a service known as the 'Kenny Belle'. These unadvertised trains between Clapham Junction and Kensington Olympia ran during weekday peak periods mainly for the benefit of Post Office staff, and until July 1967 had regularly been steam-operated. Built by the Birmingham Railway Carriage & Wagon Company and entering service in October 1960 as D6528, No 33111 was withdrawn in June 1991 as is now preserved on the Swanage Railway in Dorset. This was one of the 19 D65XX locomotives that had been converted for push-pull operation with 4TC units (used mostly between Bournemouth and Weymouth) during 1967. The line from Clapham to Kensington Olympia has seen a renaissance in more recent years, and in 2013 there is a regular service of electric trains along the route as part of the London Overground.

Below: **CLAPHAM JUNCTION** The Kent coalfield was still productive in 1976, and on Tuesday 8 June Class 45 diesel-electric locomotive No 45110 rumbles through the station with a long train of loaded coal trucks from Shepherdswell to Brent, which will be reached via Wandsworth Town, Kew Bridge, Acton Wells Junction and Dudding Hill. Built by British Railways Crewe Works and entering traffic as D73 in November 1960, No 45110 remained in service with British Rail until July 1988. By the 1980s time was running out for the Kent coalfield; Snowdown and Tilmanstone collieries both closed in 1987, and Betteshanger – the final colliery in Kent – was closed in 1989.

Above: **CLAPHAM JUNCTION** The manufacture of Portland cement at Northfleet, Kent, had started in 1846, and by the beginning of the 20th century there were nine cement works in operation beside the River Thames between Swanscombe and Gravesend. Class 47 diesel-electric locomotive No 47002 has charge of a cement train from Northfleet on Tuesday 3 August 1976; it has passed through Clapham Junction station and is heading for Wandsworth Town. No 47002 was built by Brush at Loughborough and entered service in June 1963 as D1522; it was withdrawn in June 1991. By the early 1990s output of cement from Northfleet was falling, and distribution by rail from that site ceased in 1993.

The busy scene at Clapham Junction

CLAPHAM JUNCTION A six-car train, formed of three two-car units, approaches the station on Tuesday 20 April with a service that has come from the Hounslow loop. The units are, perhaps, not quite what they seem at first glance. They were built as 2HAP units at Eastleigh in 1957 and, being intended for main-line semi-fast and stopping services, their driving trailer carriages included 1st Class accommodation and lavatories – both features not provided in suburban stock. In the mid-1970s many of the 2HAP units based at Wimbledon were downgraded to 2nd Class only and used on suburban duties; the armrests in the former 1st Class compartments were secured in the up position and the lavatories were locked out of use. Reclassified 2SAP in their new guise, these units were renumbered in the 59XX series, and were easily recognised by the frosted window of the locked-up lavatory compartment roughly in the centre of the driving trailer. When the Class 508 suburban stock came into service from 1980, the 2SAP units had their 1st Class accommodation restored and the lavatories unlocked; renumbered back into the 2HAP series, they were reallocated to Brighton, where they were used mostly on the lines along the South Coast to Portsmouth and Eastbourne.

CLAPHAM JUNCTION Photographed at the same spot on the same day, we see the more usual transport for the area's suburban travellers in 1976. 4SUB units Nos 4723 and 4295 were forming a service from Staines via Richmond when caught on camera. 4SUB units were built in quantity in the years following the Second World War, and epitomised travel to and from work for a generation of commuters. The two units seen here date from 1949-50; however, the second carriage of leading unit No 4723 is a nine-compartment trailer that was built in 1947 and used to augment a pre-war three-car unit until it was re-used as part of the new 4273 in 1950. Although withdrawals of the post-war 4SUB fleet had commenced in the early 1970s, units of this type remained a very common sight until 1981, and the final 4SUB units were withdrawn from service in September 1983.

The great way west

There had undoubtedly been something different about the Great Western Railway; it had an individualistic way of going about things – even the electric sockets fitted in its premises were to a special design that ordinary plugs would not fit; after nationalisation some individualism survived with the introduction of diesel-hydraulic rather than diesel-electric locomotives. By 1976 the Western Region was very much part of the national system, although traces of the old company could still be found in some places.

READING Opened in 1840, Reading was the temporary terminus of the railway from London until the line was extended to Bristol the following year. Known as Reading General from 1949 until 1973, this busy interchange station has been subject to a number of modifications over the years, and at the time of writing is undergoing extensive reconstruction work, including the provision of five new platforms, to increase capacity. On Saturday 22 May 1976 Class 46 diesel-electric locomotive No 46016 passes through non-stop with an express for Paignton consisting mostly of BR Standard Mark 2 stock. Built at British Railways Derby Works and entering traffic as D153 in January 1962, this locomotive was in service until December 1983. On the left, diesel-hydraulic locomotive No 1015 *Western Champion* stands at Platform 5 with an up train; a product of Swindon Works and in service from January 1963 until December 1976, *Western Champion* was preserved after withdrawal and is currently in the care of the Diesel Traction Group. Notice the enthusiasts on the platform.

In the second photograph, taken in late October 1976, Class 33 diesel-electric locomotive No 33117 heads west through Reading with a troop special working made up of BR Standard Mark 1 stock. Entering traffic in December 1960 as D6536, this locomotive was adapted for push-pull operation in May 1967 and was also preserved after withdrawal in May 1993; at the time of writing it is located at the East Lancashire Railway.

DIDCOT The BRUTE trolley was introduced in an effort to speed up the loading of parcels into trains; the loaded trolley could simply be moved to the waiting train and wheeled into the brake or parcels van to continue its journey to its intended destination. The acronym BRUTE stands for British Railways Universal Trolley Equipment; they were built on a special production line at Swindon Works and were introduced in 1964, initially on the Western Region, although they were soon to be seen across most of the network. When parcels were a significant rail traffic, the BRUTE was a great aid to prompt and efficient working, although it appears that a little too much 'brute force' may have been applied to the 'Do not bend' item seen at Didcot station in October 1976! BRUTEs were taken out of use after the demise of the Red Star parcel service in 1999. *Brian Jackson*

1976 Happenings (2)

July
- Heatwave continues; temperatures reach 97°F in Cheltenham.
- David Steel is elected leader of Liberal Party.
- Ford Fiesta launched.
- At Olympic Games in Montreal, Great Britain and Northern Ireland win three gold, five silver and five bronze medals.
- Southend Pier seriously damaged by fire.

August
- Heatwave and drought continue.
- Trade Union Congress and Government agree 'Stage 2' limit on pay rises.
- 'Big Ben' breaks down (not fully repaired until May 1977).
- Former Postmaster General John Stonehouse sentenced to seven years in prison for fraud.
- Riots at Notting Hill Carnival result in 160 people being injured, including 100 police officers.

September
- 25,000 people call for end to violence in Northern Ireland at peace march in Derry.
- Ford Cortina Mark 4 launched.

October
- British Rail introduces InterCity 125 trains on high-speed schedules (see pages 4-7).
- James Hunt becomes Formula 1 World Champion.
- Royal National Theatre opens on London's South Bank.
- Selby coalfield opens.

November
- Jimmy Carter becomes President of the United States of America.

December
- Chancellor of the Exchequer Denis Healey announces cuts in public expenditure as result of negotiating £2.3 billion loan from International Monetary Fund.

Below: **APPLEFORD** An architectural trait of the Great Western Railway was the 'pagoda' hut, erected at many halts from the early 1900s onwards. These corrugated-iron structures were not made at the company's Swindon Works, but were supplied by Messrs Taylor of Birmingham. Appleford Halt, between Didcot and Culham on the Oxford line, was opened on 11 September 1933 at a cost of £588. Like many similar halts opened around that time, it was a response to the competition that was emerging from motor buses, which were increasingly serving outlying districts. The closure of large numbers of small stations and halts, particularly as a result of the Beeching Report in the 1960s, meant that few locations with 'pagoda' shelters remained when this photograph of Appleford was taken in October 1976. In fact, the 'pagodas' survived here into the 1990s, but were then replaced by modern shelters incorporating a large amount of glazing. *Brian Jackson*

Above: **CULHAM** station, situated on the Didcot to Oxford line, opened on 12 June 1844 as Abingdon Road; it was renamed Culham on 2 June 1856, and this photograph was taken in October 1976. The Tudor-style station was designed by Brunel, and in the 21st century the surviving main building is a Grade 2 listed structure. Like many small stations, passenger numbers declined from the 1960s; however, the easy commuting distance to Oxford, Reading and London has seen the number of passengers using Culham station increase by 67% between 2006 and 2009. *Brian Jackson*

Below: **WESTBURY** With the completion of the transfer of the Class 50 diesel-electric locomotives from the London Midland Region in the spring of 1976, together with the introduction of the InterCity 125 High Speed Trains, British Rail predicted the demise of the remaining diesel-hydraulic Class 52s by the end of 1976. Nonetheless a dozen survived into the following year, and it was not until February 1977 that the withdrawal of the final five examples brought the diesel-hydraulic era to an end. But the sun was quite literally setting on the class when this photograph was taken at Westbury on an early November evening in 1976. Although they were awaiting their next turns of duty, neither locomotive would survive much longer in service; No 1053 *Western Patriarch* (left), built at Crewe in February 1963, was withdrawn on 15 November 1976, while No 1071 *Western Renown*, outshopped from Crewe in November 1963, was taken out of service on 7 December 1976. *Brian Jackson*

Below: **SWINDON** The Western Region had been unique in specifying hydraulic, rather than electric, transmission for diesel locomotives, and the Class 52 'Westerns' were perhaps the best-liked examples of this type. A total of 74 entered service between 1961 and 1964, and at the end of 1975 37 were still in service as the only remaining diesel-hydraulics in the British Rail fleet. Withdrawals were continuing, however, and on a bitterly cold December morning in 1976 five 'Westerns' await the final blow in the scrapyard at Swindon. From left to right we see Nos 1012 *Western Firebrand* (built at Swindon in November 1962), 1025 *Western Guardsman* (built at Swindon in November 1963), 1064 *Western Regent* (built at Crewe in May 1963), 1057 *Western Chieftain* (built at Crewe in April 1963), and 1028 *Western Hussar* (built at Swindon in February 1964). *Brian Jackson*

Left: **SWINDON** First opened in January 1843 as a locomotive depot and repair shop, the Great Western Works at Swindon was extended and enlarged during the 19th and early 20th centuries. Locomotive building commenced in 1846, while the carriage and wagon shops came into use in 1869. The works was turning out standard-gauge as well as broad-gauge stock, although the latter was finally eliminated in 1892. A visit to Swindon Works always provided items of interest, and seen here in 1976 is this mixed-gauge wagon turntable, believed to have been in use at the works from 1845 until 1965. *Brian Jackson*

Below left: **SWINDON** Another interesting reminder of the past seen at Swindon in December 1976 was this former GWR 16-foot-wheelbase departmental vehicle. Numbered DW17931, it is clearly designated 'Sleeping & Messing Van, London District', and appears to be in excellent condition despite being relegated to the scrap area when photographed. Built in 1913, this van must have attended some interesting events during its lifetime. *Brian Jackson*

Right: **COGLOAD** Photographed during the summer of 1976, Cogload Signal Box stands at the junction of the GWR main line from Bristol and the 1906-built 'cut-off' line from Castle Cary. Fortunately, being of timber construction it was a relatively simple matter to reposition the box, which was placed in the location seen here with the completion of the Cogload flyover in 1931. The box was subsequently closed on 5 April 1986 when the area came under the control of the Exeter panel. The following year the structure was moved to the GWR Museum at Coleford in the Forest of Dean, where it has been renamed Coleford Junction. *Brian Jackson*

Below: **BRADFORD PEVERELL & STRATTON** Originally promoted by the Wilts, Somerset & Weymouth Railway Company, which was acquired by the GWR in 1850, the line between Yeovil and Weymouth was opened in January 1857. This halt at Bradford Peverell & Stratton was opened on 22 May 1933 as a simple wooden structure. Despite having been rebuilt in concrete in 1959 and the presence of housing nearby, it was closed on 3 October 1966. Three years later the line between Castle Cary and Dorchester was singled; when photographed in 1976, although it appears that the track is alongside the old platform, it has in fact been slewed, leaving a considerable gap that remains to the time of writing. *Brian Jackson*

Above: **ATHELNEY** Situated on the 1906 'cut-off' between Castle Cary and Cogload Junction, which gave the GWR a direct route to the West Country, Athelney Signal Box is seen in January 1976. This also closed on 5 April 1986 when the Exeter panel became responsible for the area. In the 21st century the upper section of this signal box and the lever frame are incorporated into a new structure called Bishops Bridge Signal Box at Staverton on the South Devon Railway. *Brian Jackson*

UPWEY & BROADWEY Class 47 diesel-electric locomotive No 47082 approaches Upwey & Broadwey station hauling a failed diesel multiple unit on Saturday 12 June 1976. The foreground is the point at which the former Abbotsbury branch had left the main line to enter the branch platform at the station, which had opened in April 1866 and was originally known as Upwey Junction. The Abbotsbury branch was closed in November 1952, and the station was renamed Upwey & Broadwey; it became unstaffed from 1965, while the traditional buildings were replaced by austere modern shelters during the 1970s. Nonetheless, the station remains open, and in the 21st century enjoys its best ever service with hourly trains to London Waterloo daily in addition to the trains to Yeovil, Westbury and Bristol. *Brian Jackson*

No 1 Records

WEYMOUTH When the GWR opened its broad-gauge line to Weymouth in January 1857, the line south of Dorchester Junction was equipped as dual gauge so that the London & South Western Railway could also run trains over that section of line. Thus from opening Weymouth was served by trains from both Paddington and Waterloo. This route was converted entirely to standard gauge in 1874. Although services on the line from Waterloo were quicker and more frequent, a few through trains between Paddington and Weymouth via Reading, Castle Cary, Yeovil and Maiden Newton continued until September 1961. However, on Sunday 22 August 1976 a nine-car excursion made up of diesel multiple unit stock ran from Paddington to Weymouth, and is seen here after arrival at Platform 4 of the seaside terminus. Weymouth station was subsequently rebuilt in 1986 on a much smaller scale. *Brian Jackson*

January
Bohemian Rhapsody — Queen

February
Mamma Mia — Abba
Forever And Ever — Silk
December '63 — Four Seasons

March
I love to Love (But My Baby Loves to Dance) — Tina Charles

April
Save Your Kisses For Me — Brotherhood of Man

May
Fernando — Abba

June
No Charge — J. J. Barrie
Combine Harvester (Brand New Key) — Wurzels
You To Me Are Everything — Real Thing

July
Forever and Ever — Demis Roussos

August
Don't Go Breaking My Heart — Elton John & Kiki Dee

September
Dancing Queen — Abba

October
Mississippi — Pussycat

November
If You Leave Me Now — Chicago

December
Under The Moon Of Love — Showaddywaddy
When A Child is Born — Johnny Mathis

Right: **LONG MARSTON** The GWR's North Warwickshire line was opened in July 1859, Long Marston being situated two stations south-west of Stratford-upon-Avon on that route. The signal box, which was photographed early in 1976, dated from 1892 and originally contained a 25-lever frame; this was replaced in September 1936 by a 32-lever second-hand frame of unknown provenance. During the Second World War a 455-acre site next to the station became a supply depot for the Railway Operating Company, Royal Engineers, with a 45-mile railway system. Additionally, Long Marston Airfield was nearby. Closure of the station came on 3 January 1966; the signal box subsequently became a ground frame on 24 March 1980 and demolition followed in November 1989. *Brian Jackson*

Left: **TAUNTON** Class 50 diesel-electric locomotive No 50019 approaches Taunton with a down Paddington to Plymouth express early in 1976. Built by English Electric and entering service as D419 on the London Midland Region's West Coast Main Line between Crewe and Glasgow in April 1968, No 50019 had been transferred to the Western Region in 1974 with other members of the class to replace diesel-hydraulic locomotives. No 50019 was subsequently named *Ramillies* at Laira in April 1978 and was preserved after withdrawal in September 1990; at the time of writing it is operational on the Mid Norfolk Railway. *Brian Jackson*

BISHOPS LYDEARD Once the short, sharp staccato exhaust of the GWR '45XX' and '55XX' 2-6-2 tanks pulling away from stations was very much part of the West Country scene. Purchased by the West Somerset Railway Association for £14,000 including delivery, three members of the class stand at Bishops Lydeard on the then closed Minehead branch in January 1976, awaiting attention having just arrived from Barry scrapyard. After a process that for many people appeared impossible, all three have been restored. Nos 4561 and 5542 are on the West Somerset Railway, which is especially appropriate for the latter, which was a Taunton-allocated loco before the Second World War. No 5521 at the time of writing can be seen in action on the Dean Forest Railway. *Brian Jackson*

BISHOPS LYDEARD A second photograph taken on the same day in January 1976 illustrates the three locomotives recently delivered from Barry. Bishops Lydeard station and signal box can be seen in the left background of this view, which is looking towards Minehead. In 1976 the station was closed and forlorn; now it is the eastern terminus of the reopened heritage West Somerset Railway. The 20-mile ride from Bishops Lydeard to Minehead gives delightful views of the Somerset countryside and the Bristol Channel coast, and a visit is highly recommended. *Brian Jackson*

Underground interlude

RICHMOND London Transport's District Line and the London Midland Region's North London Line from Richmond to Broad Street shared tracks between Richmond and Gunnersbury, and the trains had their own terminal platforms, equipped for third and fourth rail operation, at the Southern Region's Richmond station. On Thursday 6 May 1976 a District Line train was photographed from an overtaking Reading to Waterloo service. Departing from Richmond for Dagenham East, the seven-car train is formed of Class R stock, which was in service on the District Line between 1950 and 1983.

WIMBLEDON Another location where the District Line has terminal platforms within a Southern Region suburban station is Wimbledon. The train seen arriving on Saturday 14 February consists of CO/CP stock dating from 1937-40; for many years this stock was used on the Metropolitan Line service to Uxbridge, but from 1962 onwards was cascaded to the District Line. Comfortable to travel in, and very modern-looking at the time of introduction, the last train of CO/CP stock ran in normal passenger service on the District Line on 31 March 1981.

Underground interlude

WIMBLEDON A rather more unusual Underground ensemble was photographed at Wimbledon on Thursday 22 July. London Transport battery locomotive No L45, built at British Rail Engineering Doncaster Works in 1974, hauls a former Metropolitan Railway carriage dating from 1900. This had ended its days in service on the Metropolitan Line's Chesham branch, finally being withdrawn in September 1960 when the branch was electrified. When seen here carriage No 519 was being moved from storage at Preston Park to London Transport's Ruislip depot for restoration; it was later displayed at the London Transport Museum in Covent Garden. Bringing up the rear is brake van No B555, built by the Gloucester Railway Carriage & Wagon Company for London Transport in 1935.

EDGWARE ROAD There are two nearby stations on the London Underground system carrying the name Edgware Road: one is at surface level and serves the Circle and Hammersmith & City lines together with a branch of the District Line from Earls Court, while the other is a deep-level tube station on the Bakerloo Line. The two stations are in adjacent streets, but are not physically connected. The surface-level station is seen here on Saturday 16 October; the CO/CP stock train in the foreground, dating from the late 1930s, can be compared with the 1970-built train of C69 stock just visible in the background.

full-size main-line rolling stock. Opened in 1904 as a self-contained line, ownership later passed to the Metropolitan Railway and in due course to London Transport; from the late 1930s the route was operated as a separate branch of the Northern Line. Under the Great Northern suburban electrification scheme the line from Drayton Park to Moorgate was transferred from London Transport to British Rail. The last Northern Line tube train ran on the route on 4 October 1975, and after a short closure to allow the line to be converted to 750-volt DC operation using dual-voltage Class 313 electric multiple units, and physical connection to be completed with the main-line network at Finsbury Park, the route was reopened with through trains between Hertfordshire and Moorgate from 8 November 1976. Prior to this, a shuttle service between Old Street and Drayton Park had commenced from 10 August 1976; passengers are seen boarding one of the new Class 313 electric multiple units at Old Street on Saturday 16 October.

Above: **PADDINGTON** Having travelled one stop west from Edgware Road, we come to Paddington, where we see a Circle Line train of C69 stock entering the station, also on Saturday 16 October. The Circle Line platforms at Paddington are on the opposite side of Praed Street from Paddington main-line station; Hammersmith & City trains use platforms beside the main terminus, while the Bakerloo Line is in a deep-level tube. At the time of writing the C stock on the Circle Line is the oldest remaining in regular service on the London Underground.

Right: **OLD STREET** Although a deep-level underground line from Finsbury Park to Moorgate, the Great Northern & City Railway was built with 16-foot-diameter tunnels that were able to accommodate

Nostalgia at the Bluebell Railway

HORSTED KEYNES In August 1960 the Bluebell Railway had become the first standard-gauge line closed by British Railways to be reopened by preservationists, and this early head start provided the opportunity to preserve examples of elderly railway stock that was fast disappearing from the scene by that time. Photographed on Wednesday 10 March 1976 at Horsted Keynes, this former London, Chatham & Dover Railway six-wheeled Brake dated from 1894, and had been built on a wooden, rather than the more usual metal, underframe. Withdrawn in 1935, it had become a departmental vehicle at Redbridge sleeper works, near Southampton, until 1962, when it was acquired by the Bluebell Railway for preservation. Although it initially continued in departmental use at its new home, both age and the weather have taken their toll, and at the time of writing this historic carriage is in store. *Brian Jackson*

SHEFFIELD PARK Carrying the number 21C123 allocated by the Southern Railway when it entered traffic in 1946, 'West Country' Class 'Pacific' *Blackmoor Vale* is seen beautifully restored to her original condition at Sheffield Park on Sunday 19 September 1976. *Blackmoor Vale* was one of the Bulleid 'light Pacifics' that escaped rebuilding from streamlined form in the late 1950s/early 1960s, and remained in traffic until the very end of steam on the Southern Region, being withdrawn in July 1967, by then numbered 34023. After withdrawal, the locomotive became the property of the Bulleid Society, and in due course arrived at the Bluebell Railway in late 1971. A thorough overhaul followed, and 21C123 entered traffic on the Bluebell in May 1976. This magnificent and popular locomotive saw heavy use on the line for a number of years, and is currently in store at Sheffield Park.

SHEFFIELD PARK The 'C' Class was Harry Wainwright's first steam locomotive design for the South Eastern & Chatham Railway, and was intended to meet the need for a standard goods engine. No 592 was built at the railway's Longhedge Works, Battersea, in 1902 as one of a class that numbered 109 locomotives by 1908 – the largest class on the SECR. The mainstay of goods workings across South East England, they were also used for passenger trains, including long-distance excursions and, increasingly in later life, local passenger services. When the railways were nationalised in 1948, 106 of the 'C' Class locomotives passed into British Railways ownership, including No 592, which was given the BR number 31592. However, by 1964 all of the class had been withdrawn from general traffic, although three (including No 31592, by then renumbered DS239) survived as yard shunters at Ashford Works. Taken into the ownership of the C Class Locomotive Preservation Society, No 592 arrived on the Bluebell Railway in August 1970, and entered traffic on the line in May 1975; at the time of writing it remains available for traffic, and is the last surviving locomotive built at Longhedge Works.

When photographed at Sheffield Park in March 1976, it will be noticed that the first carriage in the train is a British Railways Standard Mark 1 suburban CL dating from the mid-1950s. The Bluebell Railway bought three carriages of this type during the 1970s, which had previously been used on Eastern Region suburban services from King's Cross. They entered traffic on the Bluebell in British Rail overall blue livery, and were intended as a stopgap to allow the Bluebell's Carriage & Wagon Department to catch up on maintenance and repairs of the historic carriages that are such an important feature of that line. The three Mark 1 suburban carriages were accordingly later sold to the North Tyneside Railway, North Shields, where they can now be seen restored to their original 1950s condition in British Railways maroon livery. *Brian Jackson*

Nostalgia at the Bluebell Railway

of the restored Bluebell Railway northwards from Kingscote to East Grinstead, the line has once again been directly connected with the national rail network – indeed, Bluebell Railway trains depart from what has been designated Platform 3 at East Grinstead station. The opening of this extension makes a trip to the Bluebell Railway by public transport very easy indeed; the wonderful collection of locomotives and rolling stock on this line ensures that a visit is an extremely worthwhile and enjoyable experience, which is most highly recommended. *Both Brian Jackson*

HORSTED KEYNES signal box, photographed in 1976, was built to a London, Brighton & South Coast Railway design with equipment by Saxby & Farmer, and its 40-lever frame was in 1976 the largest operating lever frame on a preserved railway. From 1935 until closure in 1963, the branch from Haywards Heath to Horsted Keynes was electrified, the electric service running between Horsted Keynes, Haywards Heath, Lewes and Seaford. The electric trains ran into what is now Platform 2 at Horsted Keynes, and from August 1960 until October 1963 they linked the heritage Bluebell Railway with the national BR network. For almost 50 years such a link was lost, but in March 2013, with the opening

As it was in the beginning...

STRATFORD-UPON-AVON
Plateways and tramways were the forerunners of today's railways. Photographed early in 1976, a former horse-drawn wagon of the Stratford & Moreton Tramway stands in Stratford-upon-Avon on a section of original track, the rails supported by two lines of stone blocks; this arrangement allowed the horse an unobstructed walk. This standard-gauge tramway opened in 1826, with an extension to Shipston-on-Stour ten years later. The line from Shipston-on-Stour to Moreton-in-Marsh was converted to a conventional railway, operated by the GWR, in 1859; although closed to passengers in 1929, it remained open for goods traffic until 1960. The northern section of the tramway remained horse-drawn until closure during the 1880s. In 1976 a few earthworks, a multi-arch bridge over the River Avon at Stratford and the Old Tramway Inn in Shipston Road, Stratford-upon-Avon, remained to remind us of the old tramway and its place in transport history. *Brian Jackson*

A saunter round the Southern

SALISBURY The delightful city of Salisbury has a sad place in the mind of railway historians as the location of a horrific high-speed derailment during the early hours of 1 July 1906 when a Plymouth to Waterloo boat express left the rails after taking a curve at the east of the station at more than double the permitted speed. The driver was among the 28 people who tragically lost their lives, and the reason this experienced and reliable man exceeded the speed limit in such a manner has never been conclusively determined. The main station buildings illustrated here were constructed in 1900, replacing an earlier structure dating from 1857 that was still standing, out of sight in the right of this view. When photographed in November 1976 modernisation and the new corporate image had yet to impinge on the look of these fine buildings. *Brian Jackson*

NETLEY Basking in the evening sun on Thursday 12 August 1976, the exterior of Netley station had changed little over the years apart from the removal of the canopy. The scene here is a timeless one, and if we ignore the telephone kiosk and the modern posters, a good example of a Victorian station. The line from St Denys to Netley was opened on 5 March 1866, and extended to Fareham in September 1889 to form a direct line between Southampton and Portsmouth. *Brian Jackson*

GOSPORT Opened in 1841 and situated at the end of a branch from Bishopstoke (Eastleigh) on the LSWR Waterloo-Southampton main line, Gosport was the first railway station to serve Portsmouth, reached by ferry across the Harbour. Designed by Sir William Tite, an ostentatious station was provided, but the line diminished in importance a few years later when the railway reached Portsmouth in 1847. The station sustained damage during the Second World War, and was closed to passengers in June 1953, although goods traffic continued until January 1969. When photographed in August 1976, the then deteriorating Grade 2 listed structure was more reminiscent of a Greek or Roman relic than a railway passenger terminus. Various plans for the structure over the years have included use as a museum, but the Hermitage Housing Association purchased the site in 2007 and submitted a planning application for conservation, restoration and development to include housing and a community facility; the project became a winner in the prestigious Housing Design Awards 2008 demonstrating the sensitive restoration and reuse of a historic building. *Brian Jackson*

PORTSMOUTH DOCKYARD Situated at Edinburgh Road crossing on the branch serving the naval dockyard at Portsmouth, in 1976 this was the last surviving example of the early form of semaphore signal. There was no interlocking whatsoever with the gates, the arms being operated by hand levers attached to the base of the post. Although of no great age, it was an exact copy of a signal that had stood on the site for nearly 100 years and had features of the original naval semaphore telegraph. *Brian Jackson*

A saunter round the Southern

Below: **STRAWBERRY HILL** In 1897 the LSWR established a steam locomotive depot in the triangle formed by the junction of the Shepperton branch and the Kingston loop. When these lines were electrified in 1916 the premises became an electric train depot, and this was enlarged by the Southern Railway in 1936. During the early evening of Wednesday 4 February 1976 the brightly lit car sheds await the return of the suburban units after the evening peak period.

Above: **PORTSMOUTH HARBOUR** Seen alongside the Harbour station at Portsmouth during the summer of 1976, MV *Shanklin* waits to sail on the Portsmouth-Ryde passenger ferry service. Built in 1951, *Shanklin* was the youngest of three sister vessels and was equipped with two direct reversing diesel engines, whereas the other two employed gearboxes. Withdrawn during 1980, she was sold in October of that year to the Firth of Clyde Steam Packet Company, an organisation set up to assist and raise funds for PS *Waverley*, and was renamed *Prince Ivanhoe*. While cruising for her new owners in the Bristol Channel with around 400 passengers aboard on 3 August 1981, she struck an uncharted object off the Gower coast. Fortunately her master successfully ran her ashore at Horton Beach, Port Eynon, and everyone escaped from this perilous situation. Sadly the ship was a total loss, and was broken up where she lay. *Brian Jackson*

GUILDFORD Sunday journeys by rail are sometimes diverted via unusual routes to allow essential engineering and track maintenance to take place. On Sunday 23 May 1976 the 1239 Poole to Newcastle inter-regional train ran via Fareham, Liphook and Blackwater between Southampton and Reading. For this stage of the journey the train of BR Standard Mark 1 stock was double-headed by electro-diesel locomotive No 73131, which entered traffic as E6038 in August 1966 and remained in service until August 2003, and diesel-electric locomotive No 33107. The latter was built in 1960 as D6520; rebuilt for push-pull operation in May 1967, it was withdrawn in May 1989.

GUILDFORD Passengers travelling on this train to Waterloo via Cobham on Saturday 13 November were provided with an unusual hybrid unit; the two carriages nearest the camera are of main-line 4CIG design, while the rear two are of the high-density 4VEP type. The unit number 7836 suggests a standard 4VEP, but the explanation for this mixed formation was an accident that took place at Guildford on Thursday 19 August 1976. That evening 4VEP No 7836 had been part of an empty stock train being shunted, and had collided with the 1754 Waterloo to Portsmouth Harbour service as the latter was crossing from the down main to Number 2 Platform line, sadly causing injuries to seven passengers on the Portsmouth train. Damage was caused to the leading two carriages of No 7836, resulting in their temporary replacement by a couple of 4CIG carriages to keep the unit in service while repairs were carried out.

NORTH CAMP The Class 37 diesel-electric locomotives built by English Electric between 1960 and 1965 have proved to be a successful and long-lived design. This example, No 37268, was photographed at North Camp on Wednesday 8 December 1976. Entering traffic in February 1965 as D6968, this locomotive was renumbered in 1973 under the TOPS scheme, and was subsequently again renumbered to become 37401 in 1985. By October 2010 it was in store with EWS, and was officially withdrawn in March 2013.

SANDHURST A week earlier than the photograph taken at Guildford on the opposite page, we again see the diverted 1239 Poole to Newcastle train, but a little further on its journey at Sandhurst. Two Class 33 diesel-electric locomotives double-head the train on Sunday 16 May. No 33109, leading, was new in October 1960 as D6525; converted for push-pull operation in October 1967, it was preserved after withdrawal in 2001 and now resides on the East Lancashire Railway, a long way from the Bournemouth to Weymouth line on which it worked for many years in push-pull mode. The second locomotive is No 33114; this entered traffic in November 1960 as D6532, was converted for push-pull operation in May 1967, and withdrawn in February 1993.

WIMBLEDON When the LSWR commenced operating suburban electric trains from Waterloo in 1915, current was supplied from a specially constructed generating station at Durnsford Road, Wimbledon; cleaning and maintenance sheds for the electric trains were also provided on this site. By the 1960s the generating station was no longer required, arrangements having been made to obtain traction current from the National Grid, and the disused power house buildings were demolished in 1965. The 1915 car sheds were replaced by new buildings on the former generating station site; a separate building containing staff accommodation and a canteen was also provided. Known as Wimbledon East, the new depot came into use on 29 April 1974, and is seen here just over 30 months later on Friday 5 November 1976.

TV favourites

I, Claudius
Derek Jacobi won a BAFTA Best Actor award for his title role in this highly acclaimed drama series set in Ancient Rome. Other star names in the cast included John Hurt, Brian Blessed and Stratford Johns.

The Duchess of Duke Street
This 'rags to riches' serial about a maid who eventually ended up running a London hotel starred Gemma Jones and attracted large audiences.

A Bouquet of Barbed Wire
Starring Frank Finlay and Susan Penhaligon, this rather dark serial portrayed the effects of incest in a middle-class Home Counties family, and generated high viewing figures.

The Fall and Rise of Reginald Perrin
Reginald Perrin, played by Leonard Rossiter, was a middle-aged office worker for a fictional company called 'Sunshine Desserts'. He commuted by train, and each morning entered the office with a comment like 'Eleven minutes late – defective points at Raynes Park'. The main catchphrase from the show was uttered by 'CJ' (Reggie Perrin's manager), who frequently reminded people, 'I didn't get where I am today without…'

Open All Hours
This brilliant comedy series starred Ronnie Barker as a tight-fisted shopkeeper, with David Jason as his down-trodden nephew Granville. The theme music was a revised version of the old tune 'Alice, where art thou?'.

Sailor
A behind-the-scenes look at life on the high seas as a BBC team joined the crew of HMS *Ark Royal*. Rod Stewart's *Sailing* was the theme tune.

Children enjoyed *The Muppet Show*, and also *Just William* – in which a young Bonnie Langford played Violet Elizabeth Bott, threatening to 'thcweam and thcweam until she was thick' if things did not go her way. (Violet's mother, Mrs Bott, was played by Diana Dors.)

A saunter round the Southern

Right: **WADHURST** The history of railway signalling is long and complex, especially in the early years when various manufacturers vied with each other to provide the best and most up-to-date equipment. Lever frames constructed by Messrs Dutton were never a common sight on the railways of Southern England; in 1976 this 22-lever example at Wadhurst on the former SECR Hastings line was the sole survivor. *Brian Jackson*

Below: **TUNBRIDGE WELLS WEST** On a dull Sunday in March 1976 Tunbridge Wells West station has something of an allure of the macabre about it. Although the platforms have modern electric lamps, the old green totem station nameplates have been retained, while the station building is lit by hissing gas lamps and has not seen a coat of paint for years. A casual observer could be forgiven for thinking that he had wandered into something of a time-warp, but the blue-liveried diesel-electric multiple units are another reminder that this is indeed 1976. The station was situated on the former LB&SCR Tunbridge Wells-Eridge line and had opened on 1 October 1866. This line was subsequently closed to all traffic on 6 July 1985, but has since been reopened by preservationists as the Spa Valley Railway; on operating days it is again possible to travel by train from Tunbridge Wells West to Eridge, although the development of a supermarket on the site means that a new platform has been provided for the heritage service at Tunbridge Wells West. Nonetheless, the line is a delightful one with preserved stock from both steam and diesel eras, and well worth a visit. *Brian Jackson*

Acknowledgements

It would not have been possible to produce this book without making use of the photograph collections of Ray Ruffell and Brian Jackson.

The late Ray Ruffell was a railwayman by profession, but his interest in transport went far beyond his day-to-day work. He travelled widely during his off-duty time and created a photographic record of many parts of the railway system during a period when great change was under way. These photographs are now in the safe keeping of The NOSTALGIA Collection, forming a significant part of the company's photographic archive.

Transport historian Brian Jackson also travelled extensively with his camera to record the ever-changing transport scene. He has been kind enough to allow me to use many photographs that he took during 1976 and which are credited individually within the book; my warm thanks for his cheerful and willing help.

Many scenes that were everyday and commonplace when Ray or Brian photographed them have now been swept away for ever, and the memories captured on film, precious at the time, are now beyond price.

I would like to say a sincere thank you to the team at The NOSTALGIA Collection for inviting me to write this book. The cheerful and willing help I have received from Peter Townsend, David Walshaw and Will Adams has been very much appreciated, and I feel deeply honoured to work with such kind people.

I hope you have enjoyed this look back at 1976 and that you will want to sample more years in the 'Railways & Recollections' series.

Index

General
Bluebell Railway 37-39
BRUTE trolleys 25
'Kenny Belle' 21
MV *Shanklin* 43
Stratford & Moreton Tramway 40
Trent Motor Traction garage, Derby 13

Locations
Appleford 26
Athelney signal box 29
Bishops Lydeard 33
Bradford Peverell & Stratton 29
Cannington Viaduct 8
Chard Junction 17-19; Central 19
Chester 1
Chippenham 5
Clapham Junction 21-23
Cogload signal box 29
Combpyne 9
Crediton 20
Culham 26
Derby 10-13
Didcot 25
Edgware Road 35
Gosport 42
Guildford 44
Horsted Keynes 37, 39
Long Marston signal box 32
Lyme Regis 8
Meldon Quarry 20
Netley 41
Newport 6
North Camp 45
Old Street 36
Paddington 6; Circle Line 36
Portsmouth Dockyard 42
Portsmouth Harbour 43
Reading 4-5, 24
Richmond 34
Salisbury 41
Sandhurst 45
Sheffield Park 37, 38
Stratford-upon-Avon 40
Strawberry Hill 43
Swindon 27, 28
Taunton 32
Tunbridge Wells West 47
Upwey & Broadwey 30
Wadhurst signal box 47
Waterloo 14-16
Westbury 27
Weymouth 31
Wimbledon 34-35, 46
Windsor & Eton Riverside 3

Locomotives, diesel
Class 08 10
Class 25 12
Class 33 17, 21, 24, 44, 45
Class 37 45
Class 45 12, 13, 22
Class 46 24
Class 47 22, 30
Class 50 32
Class 52 'Western' 4, 20, 24, 27
United Dairies shunter No 12 18

Locomotives, electro-diesel
Class 73 44
Class 74 15

Locomotives, steam
1708 (MR 1F 0-6-0T) 12
21C123 (SR 4-6-2) 37
4561 (GWR 2-6-2T) 33
5542 (GWR 2-6-2T) 33
592 (SECR 0-6-0) 38

London Underground
Battery loco L45 35
C69 stock 35, 36
CO/CP stock 34, 35
R stock 34

Multiple units, diesel
Class 104 10
Class 119 17
Class 120 10
Class 253 (InterCity 125 HST) 4-7

Multiple units, electric
2EPB 21
2HAP/SAP 23
4CIG 14, 44
4EPB 16
4PEP 14
4SUB 23
4VEP 16, 44
Class 313 36